BREAKING THROUGH
TO THE REAL YOU

The Three Most Powerful Wonders Within You

BY KWAME FRIMPONG

What a powerful and necessary book! Kwame Frimpong's book "Breaking Through to The real You" is a classic handbook written out of decade of experience. This book is a burden remover. It will lift you up and encourage you to fulfill God's plan for your life.

Dr Akwasi Sintim
Professor of Philosophy and Apologetics
Raleigh NC

An extraordinary book that deals with the question, "How can I discover my spiritual gift?" You no longer have to worry anymore about your gift.

This book is a giant forward in knowing and using the gift God has given to us regardless of the barriers around you.

David and Dawn Spittle
Real Estate Broker
Raleigh, NC

I highly recommend this book. It has been written by an anointed young man of God who is also a good friend of mine. You will experience the anointing of God greatly in your life as you apply the application of these truths in your life. Breaking through to the real you is a wonderful book for the body of Christ.

Amos Toe
President
Ecowas Forest Bureau

BREAKING THROUGH TO THE REAL YOU

By Kwame Frimpong

ISBN: 978-1499161380
ISBN-10: 1499161387

Library of Congress Control Number: 2008907733

DEDICATION

I would like to dedicate this book to my precious pearl, my spouse Mary, who is God's true helpmate to me. She has been a constant source of encouragement, support and inspiration. She has given me the freedom to pursue my purpose in life. I also dedicate this book to my three daughters Esther, Gloria, and Edna. Finally, I would like to dedicate this book to the source and sustainer of life, the all-powerful God and my personal Savior, the Lord Jesus Christ.

TABLE OF CONTENTS

I can never give the Lord praise enough for letting me have the privilege of reading Pastor Kwame Frimpong's book "Breaking Through To The Real You".

Pastor Kwame Frimpong, a great teacher an expositor of the Word of God has made the discovering of spiritual gifts very easy. As you read this book, you would no longer be ignorant of your spiritual gift or confused about your purpose. This book will serve as an eye opener to you as you pursue the will of God for your life.

If you have experienced the blows of the enemy and you really want to get up and see the reality of the purpose of God in your life, then this book is for you. While reading this book I "caught" a whole new understanding of gifts I never knew that I had. Now I feel like heaven has been opened unto me with a fresh new start as God through this book has opened my eyes to what I never knew before.

I could never put this book down, I would read a few minutes, then stop and meditate on God's plan for me then read some more. I felt as though someone was just sitting close to me pointing to me all the blessings of God in my life I have not tapped into yet. I recommend that you read every word of this book. Let the Holy Ghost help you to open your hearts as He shows you the power of your natural flow.

This book is for those who need a fresh start in their lives, those who desire to breakthrough into new heights and affect their generations with a clear cut understanding of the purpose of God for their lives. Now read and breakthrough now!

Thank you, my friend Pastor Kwame Frimpong.

Amos Toe
President
Ecowas Forest Bureau
Alexandria, VA

PREFACE

Are you living the abundant life? Or do you feel like the driver who took a wrong turn and never found his way back to the main road? Perhaps you believe your life is destined for better things, but somewhere you have lost your way. It seems life has become too busy, too complex, and too demanding for you to pursue your dreams or develop your talents. Instead of aiming for the stars, have you settled for surviving whatever life throws at you?

As a child of God, you are destined for great things on this earth. You do not have to settle for merely surviving day to day until you draw your last breath. I realized many years ago my destiny is to help people discover their purpose in life. It is what I enjoy doing. In fact, I cannot stop myself from trying to help people become what God intended them to be. You will find your way in this life by discovering who you are and by exercising the gifts within you. Many people are unhappy today because they do not know who they are, and therefore, they do not recognize their own potential. If you are ready to discover the real person God made you to be, then this book is for you.

My friend, I wrote this book to bring you good news: God wants you to live the abundant life. He wants you to be free from the hurts of the past. Jesus said, "The thief comes only to steal and kill and destroy: I have come that they may have life, and have it to the full" (John10:10). Our Lord could not have spoken his purpose more plainly. He did not say He wants us to endure a life with resources barely sufficient to meet our needs. He never instructed us to muddle through life, hoping for the best, but expecting the worst. He used the word "full" for a reason. Jesus desires us to overflow with life so we may be a blessing to others.

Although God's plan for us is clear, I am concerned that many good and decent people will have an unpleasant surprise awaiting them in heaven. Of course they will rejoice when they realize they are in heaven, but when given an opportunity to see their earthly life through the lens of heaven, they will be greatly disappointed. Many will be shocked to see what God had planned for them and wonder how they missed. Perhaps it will be like watching an epic movie entitled, "Your Abundant Life," with a central figure that does heroic deeds. About half way through the film, the person newly arrived in heaven exclaims, "What's going on? That's me in the movie, but this wasn't my life! You mean God wanted me to have so much more than what I settled for? So much more than I thought was possible?"

Many people are going to realize one day that it was not devils or demons that stopped them from realizing their full potential. The devil did not have to do anything bad to them; they just limited themselves by denying the power of God in their lives. Their wrong thinking was their own devil. Their thinking was wrong because they never seriously challenged the negative influences around them with the Word of God. You do not have to be one of these disappointed souls. You can be one to whom Jesus says, "Well done, good and faithful servant."

My friend, walk with me through this book as we break the chains of negative thinking and influences in your life to discover the real you.

INTRODUCTION

Have You Ever Felt Like Where You Are In Life Is Not Where You Feel You Should Be?

"Pastor, something just isn't right with my life."

Let us begin by asking several questions. Does your heart tell you that where you are in your life is not quite where you are supposed to be? Some experts advise us not to compare ourselves to others and that is usually good advice. But, comparing yourself against your potential is not wrong. Looking at where you are in relation to where you can be is a liberating experience. We are encouraged to reach higher when we realize the goal is certainly within our grasp. Have you ever felt that you could do more or you could do better? If this is your cry, it is a good desire because God wants you to live an abundant life instead of a mediocre life.

Perhaps you are outwardly successful, but you are still not fulfilled. That brings to mind the question, what is fulfillment? It is a yearning to be whole; it is a silent joy in the soul of an individual. Satisfaction is an inside work therefore, everyone can achieve it. Do you feel as though something is missing? A certain young man came to me after I preached one night. He was crying, and he said to me, "Pastor, I have a good job, but I am not happy in my Christian life. Something just isn't right. Please pray for me." Before I prayed, I felt the Lord wanted me to tell him that he was neglecting to do something God wanted him to do. His eyes opened wider with a look of recognition, as if this word confirmed what he already knew. Several weeks later he called me with good news: he was feeling great because he was doing something that was connected to his calling. He was starting to flow with his natural gifts and abilities, and his strength was renewed. Praise the Lord!

"You don't know what I have been through!"

The devil is keeping many Christians in the prison of their past. Past mistakes and experiences can keep you from fulfilling your dreams. Often we let the past deprive us of our today and tomorrow. I once asked a pastor to help me do something that he was uniquely qualified for. His angry reaction surprised me. For some reason he remembered all the times that people had misused him. "You don't know what I have been through and how people have treated me," he explained. "I have decided never to get involved in that work again." How unfortunate this is! The Kingdom of God is missing out on this man's gift because of his inability to let go of the past.

Are you allowing the past to dictate for you? I have good news for you. I encourage you to learn from the past but please understand that your past is not your personal guide and teacher. The past cannot save your life, but God can. The past cannot forgive you, but God will. Ask God to show you what you need to learn from the past, and then move on to the unique person he created you to be.

You already know why God put you here.

You did not pick up this book because you expected it to be a mystery novel, so I assume you will not be disappointed that I am going to erase all suspense at this moment to tell you a simple truth: you already know the reason God placed you on this earth. This book is not a manual of rituals to perform in order to produce some mysterious message from above. There are no magic formulas or codes presented here. God does not place puzzles in front of us, hoping we can somehow figure them out. When God speaks to me, he usually uses simple, direct thoughts that are often a confirmation of what I already know in my spirit. You know deep in your spirit and mind the reason you are here.

Your destiny, your purpose, is not something you go out and manufacture. You do not decide to fulfill your destiny. Instead, you discover your destiny. Think of the word this way: dis-cover, to take the covers off of our eyes and see clearly. What you were destined to do has been in you from birth, but it has been covered by your environment. Perhaps you are a natural musician, but someone told you early in life, "there is no money in playing the piano, kid, so forget about piano lessons." You may have lived in a very critical family that gave you punishment but never any praise, and therefore, you covered your gift in order to protect yourself. Some parents with good intentions fail to recognize their child's special abilities until he or she is an adult. You may have stopped the natural flow of your gift by refusing to believe those who encouraged you to exercise your gift. I know a teenager who has a natural talent for sculpture. Give him some clay, and he creates a magnificent racing horse. But if someone tells him he should develop his talent for sculpture, he shrugs it off and prefers to play video games. This young man is neglecting the gift within him, but the gift is still there, waiting to be discovered.

Great teachers do not decide to teach; they discover they are teachers. The same is true for caring nurses, persuasive lawyers, talented artists, nurturing pastors, and gifted speakers. Every career requires training, experience, and hard work; however, all the training in the world cannot cause a person to flow naturally in his or her gift. Your natural abilities have already been decided upon by God. You can learn to perform many types of jobs, and all honest work is honorable. But who you are and what you are destined to do is already written in God's good plans. You just need to uncover those plans and bring them to pass on earth so we all can be blessed by you.

God's plans for you are always good.

One way people cover or cloud their destiny is to believe the lie that God has planned something bad for them. They fear what God might have in store for them, so they avoid any discussion of discovering something better than their current drudgery. A young mother who struggled for decades in low-wage jobs once told me, "I know I will never achieve my dreams because I was born under the sign of a bad planet." This type of thinking will keep that woman's true abilities buried forever if she does not toss that lie back to the pit where it belongs. Superstitious and fatalistic beliefs such as hers are actually a convenient way for her to avoid the challenge that comes with leaving her comfort zone, stretching her spiritual muscles, and discovering her true potential.

We should rejoice over God's plans for us because they are always good. Again, I am removing all suspense: God's plans for you are for good and not for bad. The letter of James is clear about what awaits you: "Every good gift and every perfect gift is from above, and cometh down from the Father of lights, with whom is no variableness, neither shadow of turning" (James 1:17).

Jesus told us to pray "Thy kingdom come, Thy will be done in earth, as it is in heaven" (Matthew 6:10). Instead of planning to leave the earth and go to heaven, we should be praying God's will for our lives to be done here so we might bring his kingdom to earth through us. God told Moses to be careful to build the tabernacle according to the vision he showed him on the mountain. The plan for the tabernacle was already there in great detail in the mind of God. He gave Moses the task of building that magnificent structure on earth (Exodus 20). God's plans in heaven are good plans, and he wants to manifest those plans through you here on earth. That is why you feel so much energy when you are exercising your gift. Together, you and God can bring light where there was darkness, structure where there was chaos, and joy where there was sadness.

***YOUR STRENGTH CAN
BE SHARPENED GREATLY BY
HOW MUCH YOU
ARE COMMITTED TO IT***

QUESTIONS TO PONDER

What do I want to do?

What do I want to become?

What contribution do I want to make?

What do I want to spend my time with?

How much time do I want off for fun?

Considering the last twelve months on your life, how much difference did you make toward your destiny?

What plans do I have in place right now to make a difference in my life?

Your mind is a

It works best when it's open up

Chapter I

THE POWER OF YOUR NATURAL FLOW

How do you discover your brilliance, your gifts, and your destiny? Let's examine some of the things you are doing now. If you are like most people today, your work and your life require you to perform many different tasks. You have discovered in doing some of these tasks, you are average. You are able to perform these tasks, but they do not excite you, and you know there are others who perform these duties much more naturally and creatively than you do. An average singer may do an average job of singing "Amazing Grace." A gifted singer breathes life into the same song, causing her audience to feel the emotion of the words written centuries ago by a former slave trader who found forgiveness in Jesus.

There are some endeavors we are simply not suited for. No matter how hard we try, we are useless at doing some things. I once tried to become a car salesman. My job was to sell shiny, new cars. Sounds simple enough, doesn't it? The dealership trained me repeatedly for months to no avail. I failed to sell even one car. Finally, my boss called me into his office and said, "Kwame, you are very religious. You are a good man. You have good character. But this is just not for ut he still fired me because I could not sell cars. ld have forced myself to try car sales again, but aged to sell a few cars, I would still be a pastor and a Bible teacher struggling to be a car salesman. God has called me to help people appreciate their gifts, not to sell them cars.

There is something you do that requires no struggle. It is just like water flowing downstream; you cannot stop it. You don't think about it; it's just part of who you are. For me, it is helping others to reach their potential. I do this all the time. I often ask people what they are doing, what is their passion, and what can I do to help them reach their potential. It does not matter who it is. If I were to meet the President of the United States, I would ask him what I could do to help him find his purpose on this earth and use his gifts more effectively. I cannot take away this desire to help. It is part of me. I do not have to fast and pray or memorize Bible verses in order to have this gift within me. God did not require me to recite specific prayers or go on a pilgrimage to a sacred place before I could have this gift. It is already there.

Ask yourself, "What is it I do naturally, easily and without any struggle?"

It is so natural you might miss it. It is so normal that you can easily take your eyes off of it; just like the young sculptor who doesn't hear others telling him he is talented and destined to become a great artist someday. His father sees the boy is already a sculptor, but the boy chooses to focus on other things. Many people are still struggling in life because they have taken their eyes off of the very thing they do so beautifully and easily, and they are competing with other people in fields that are foreign to them. For me, struggling to sell cars was like moving to a foreign country. It did not feel like home.

A man seeking to copy the success of healing evangelist Oral Roberts can go out and organize large choirs, publicize his meetings, and try to conduct healing services just as Oral used to do. But if there is no natural flow in the gift of healing, this man's attempt will end in frustration. What amazes me about Oral was his natural way of speaking and praying for the sick. Healers are sometimes thought of as people who shout or speak in a strange tone of voice, but not Oral. He just flowed naturally in the gift he had been given, although at times the needs of the sick seemed overwhelming, and praying for thousands of people left him exhausted.

Nature teaches us about natural abilities

Jesus used our natural world to illustrate spiritual truths. We can learn a great deal about our potential by looking at the creation. I read about a type of fish, the sailfish, which can swim almost 40 miles per hour. That is unbelievable. In the twinkling of an eye, the fish zooms far away, disappearing as if by magic. Can we chase that fish, even if we try hard? Of course not. How did the sailfish learn to swim so fast? They did not attend swimming school or motivational seminars on how to be faster fish. Their parents did not teach them how to swim. They swim because they were born to swim. It's natural for them. The birds fly and navigate their course across thousands of miles because God built them with their own navigation system.

You see others flowing in their gifts every day

Just like the amazing sailfish, other people around you are succeeding and flowing in their gifts. Many people subscribe to cable television and pay forty-five dollars per month or more to watch others who are discovering their potential. Michael Jordan seemed to float effortlessly across the basketball court on our TV screens. Comedian Chris Rock is paid to use his gift of making people laugh. What is your gift? Do people love to be around you because you make them laugh? Then make them laugh. Do your friends trust you when a crisis hits? Then comfort those who mourn. I know people who have the gift of tears. These are the precious brothers and sisters who you might not see every day, but if there is a death or serious accident in your family, they are the first ones to call or come over to your house. They don't offer empty words when you are in mourning. Most of them say very little in times of grief. They know their presence and love says it all. The Apostle Paul told us to "Rejoice with them that do rejoice, and weep with them that weep" (Romans 12:15). You are walking past people every day who need what you can give. When are you going to start flowing in your gift?

JOSEPH'S GIFTS CHANGED HIS FAMILY AND HIS NATION

When you discover your gift and begin flowing naturally in it, nothing will be able to stop you. In fact, the gift will thrive in the midst of great opposition. Joseph lived in a house full of brothers who hated him for his ability to dream and because their father, Jacob, loved Joseph more than all of his children. Eleven of Joseph's brothers hated him and did not even speak to him except in anger. Imagine living in the same house with eleven people who are plotting against you. I don't think I could ever sleep in that house, but Joseph did.

When Joseph went to bed, he did not have to pray, "Lord, please give me another dream." He just dreamed because it was natural for him. It was only natural for a young boy to rise up from his bed and tell his older brothers about his dreams: "And Joseph dreamed a dream, and he told it to his brethren: and they hated him yet the more" (Genesis 37: 5). Nothing the brothers did to him stopped Joseph from dreaming. Their threats and insults did not change the fact that Joseph was a dreamer. After young Joseph told them of dreams in which he was to be elevated above them, they even planned to kill him, throw him in a pit, and tell their parents a wild animal had eaten him. Joseph's brother Rueben convinced them not to kill him, but rather to strip him of his multicolored robe and throw him in the pit. The brothers later sold Joseph to a passing caravan of Ishmaelites for twenty pieces of silver. They sold their own brother into slavery because they could not endure hearing of his dreams (Genesis 37). But even that was not the end of Joseph and his dreams. The Ishmaelites took Joseph to Egypt and sold him to Potiphar, one of Pharaoh's officials. Potiphar's wife falsely accused Joseph of a sexual assault, and Potiphar threw Joseph into prison without a trial.

Two fellow inmates told Joseph of a dream they had. Joseph immediately gave them his interpretation. He did not have to pray and fast and struggle to get the interpretation. If any man had an excuse to retire from his ministry, it was Joseph. He was rejected and sold into slavery by his brothers; his master's wife made passes at him, and now he was an innocent man in prison with no attorney to assist him. But none of these severe injustices stopped Joseph from quickly explaining the meaning of the dream. The interpretation just flowed. As he flowed in his gift, promotion soon followed. Within two years, Pharaoh was calling on Joseph to interpret a dream of his own. When Joseph was not dreaming, he was interpreting the dreams of others and becoming elevated all the more. In the end, Pharaoh put Joseph in charge of the entire land of Egypt (Genesis 41:41).

Joseph was a unique man. He prospered wherever he found himself. No act of rejection or treachery could stop his ministry of dreams. Other people had the gift of dreaming and interpreting dreams. Joseph did not invent the concept of hearing from God in dreams. But he was the one people called for when they wanted to get a correct interpretation. Even people who did not respect Joseph's religion still respected his gift, and they knew he used it with integrity.

You are also a unique person. In all of human history, there has never been a person exactly like you. Someone else might be able to do similar things, but they cannot do them exactly as you do. How many times have we heard people remark when a great athlete retires, "We will never see another player like him." Although we will not see another player identical to our retired hero, we will see many others with their own style and grace.

The greatest struggle of your life is to discover your gifts and exercise them in the face of opposition. It may take some people years to know their gift; that is why you will need to read this book very carefully. I do not want you to spend the rest of your life doing something that is not fulfilling though you give it all your best.

Your natural gift is there without your effort

Birds are built to fly. Fish are made to speed through the oceans. You were born with an ability to do something that comes naturally for you. You may have never developed that skill, but it is still in you. Joseph was interpreting dreams from the time he was a child. David fought and killed the giant Goliath by using his natural inclination to run toward, not away from, his greatest challenges.

David was a natural runner. He did not have to fast and pray in order to run. He didn't hire a track coach to teach him how to run. David and 400 of his men ran after their enemies while 200 men stayed behind because they were too tired to go any farther (1 Samuel 30:9-10). As a teenager, David even ran after lions and bears that tried to steal lambs from his father's flock of sheep (1 Samuel 17:34-36). David explained this to King Saul when he was trying to convince Saul he could take on Goliath. "King Saul," he said, "I have been fighting and killing bears and lions since I was a kid; Goliath is just another one of those predators, and the Lord will deliver me from him, too!" King Saul immediately realized David was not bluffing. The King gave David his armor and a helmet, saying, "Go, and the Lord be with thee" (1 Samuel 17:37). What else could he say in the presence of such confidence? On the battlefield, when David saw Goliath coming toward him, what do you think he did? He ran toward him and killed him with a stone from his slingshot; he didn't even need a sword or armor to overcome this giant who had terrorized the people of Israel (1 Samuel 17:48-50).

Your gift produces great results

Joseph's interpretation of dreams led him to become a prime minister. David's killing of Goliath set a platform for his kingship. Where do you produce the greatest results in your life? Natural flow will produce extraordinary results.

You will notice that when you begin to use your gift, a great excitement will result. I placed an ad in the newspaper for a minister of music. Many people called in response to the advert but the minister we hired was one of the finest people I have ever worked with. He had not been fulfilling his ministry of music for a period of about three years due challenges that he was facing. He took the position and was doing great. One day he told me, "Pastor, my wife says she hasn't seen me this excited in years, and it's all because I am working here as your minister of music."

God wants us to be pleased and excited with the work we are doing. Look at what he did after each day of creation. He created light, and saw that it was good (Genesis 1:4). He created the dry land and the seas, and "saw that it was good" (Genesis 1: 9). There must have been excitement in the heart of God as he created each beautiful and majestic thing in our world.

My breakthrough came when I started writing

I had been struggling with many things when I met my friend, encourager, and editor at a restaurant one day. I had not seen Robby in several months. He had also been struggling with how to tell me something that was on his heart. As we began to talk about destiny, he said something to me that was very strong, comforting, and encouraging. "Kwame, if you stick to pastoring a church, you will struggle a lot, but if you turn to writing books in addition to the church, it will be more fulfilling." Robby explained that the first time he saw me on TV, he would have ordered all three of my books if I had them ready back then. This was a great blessing to me.

A few months after my meeting with Robby, I went to Alexandria, Virginia, to preach. My friend Amos gave me a ride from my sister's house to the church. Amos began to talk about what God had put on his heart concerning me. "If you will share your experiences and teachings in writing, I am convinced it will help the body of Christ worldwide," Amos said. "The grace of God is on your life, and God is directing you to write these things down. Please do not deviate from this calling." (Thank you, brother Amos, for this wonderful encouragement and confirmation.)

I was so full of joy the day I discovered that writing was one of my major gifts. I had been spending too much time on other things, struggling to make them work. When I began to write down my thoughts, they seemed to flow effortlessly. The battles in my heart ceased. I had never felt such freedom. As I was writing this, my second book, the idea for the third book came to me. That is what happens when a well of creativity is opened up inside you. It has been waiting a long time to be expressed, and just like water that has been suddenly released from a dam, it floods over dry places, bringing life and causing a huge change in the environment.

Many people have surprised me with their comments about another outlet of my ministry, my TV programs. They have said that I am very good with TV and that my voice is "radio quality." A woman who has directed a choir for one of the large churches in Raleigh for more than 20 years told me she closes the choir rehearsal early on Thursday nights so she can get home just to listen to me. Another person said that if he could just figure out how to program his VCR, he would tape all of my programs. All of these comments are a blessing to me because I have never had any professional training in telecommunications. I have not used any special music on my programs, invited any famous guests, or produced any fancy computer graphics. I only have a desire to communicate the love of Jesus.

Your breakthrough will affect others around you

I felt led to give a copy of my first book, "Overcoming Offenses," to my neighbor. I did not ask her for any money. After she read the book, she returned and brought a check for $500.00. "This is to help you get the book published," she explained. She then told my wife that the book needs to be published internationally because the world needs what is in it.

Young people need elders to help them discover their gifts

We all need the help of others to encourage us, but young people especially need adults to help them discover the gifts and brilliance already within them. So many children have no one to affirm the good in them.

Contrary to many graduation speeches, children and adults cannot be anything they want to be. "Train up a child in the way he should go, and when he is old, he will not depart from it." (Proverbs 22:6)

I used to think this verse was an instruction for parents to be strict with their children. Now I know that it means something else entirely. As a father, I need to recognize the natural talents and gifts within my children and encourage them to nurture those gifts. I will not send my children out into the world with a pat on the back and tell them to go be whatever they want to be. That is a nice-sounding slogan, but it simply is not realistic. Anyone who faces the arrows of the devil armed with nothing more than platitudes about reaching for the stars is going to be a frustrated soul. The United States Army had a better slogan, "Be all you can be." Now that is getting closer to the truth: be all you can be. There are some things you simply cannot do. There are other things you can do, but they come only with lots of struggle and straining. Then there are those things you are uniquely suited for, and you need to develop those gifts to the fullest.

EMBRACING YOUR GREATEST STRENGTH

In order to increase satisfaction in life and becoming more productive, you need to zero into the very core of your gifts. Write down the three greatest gifts in your life that are evident. To make it easier allow me to use some Bible characters to show you. The question that one should ask himself or herself is, "Which strength do I pursue?" Multiple strengths are a common dilemma. It may take time, prayers and a deep soul search together with the advice from this book to zero in on your greatest strength. Are we saying that you should stop everything that you are doing? No. You will rather begin to major on your major strength by spending more time fulfilling your very God given destiny.

JOSEPH'S THREE GIFTS

First let us take Joseph for example. Joseph had three gifts; the first was the gift of dreaming, followed by the gift of interpretation, and also the gift of administration. A lot of people knew Joseph was always dreaming, and his brothers even used to call him "the dreamer." Joseph, however, dreamed only two dreams in his lifetime; he interpreted dreams only two times, but right from his childhood, Joseph was always seen organizing or administering. He did this in his father's house, Potiphar's house, and finally he became the greatest steward or administrator in Egypt.

Now you may say, how can I know which gift comes first in my life? By failing to make this decision you will major on your minor. This situation could lead frustration and unhappiness in life. In order to do this, we would go back to what I said earlier, and that is to write down the three greatest gifts in your life. The next thing you should do is to ask yourself this question:

WHICH OF THESE THREE GIFTS DO PEOPLE DEMAND GREATLY?

1 Kings 10:23 "And all the earth sought to Solomon, to hear his wisdom which God had put in his heart." Often when people visit a king, they go to see the beauty of his kingdom, how many servants he has and the bigness of his kingdom. This was the reason why the Queen of Sheba came to King Solomon,

"And when the Queen of Sheba had seen all of Solomon's wisdom and the house that he had built and the meat of his table, and the sitting of his servants, and the attendants of his ministers and their apparel, and his cupbearers and his ascent by which he went up into the house of the Lord, there was no more spirit in her" 1 Kings 10:4-5. It is only this one time that we have a record of people coming to the King because of his possessions. The rest of the people who came to see King Solomon came because they wanted to hear words of wisdom from him. There was a great demand for this gift. The majority of the people who followed Jesus did so because they needed healing in their physical bodies. I always put it this way: Jesus himself did not tell people to touch his garment for healing, but the people themselves pulled the anointing from him so much that they began to just touch him. Which of your gifts do people demand greatly?

Things to remember

You can do all things through Christ however, to be more productive focus on your great gift.

Vision is what makes you like yourself regardless, Favor is what makes people like you regardless and grace is what makes God like you regardless.

Repot your talent- to transplant a plant to a bigger pot so it is not root bound and the roots have no room to grow.

Make room for innovation.

QUESTIONS TO ANSWER

What gifts, skills, abilities and talents do I have right now?

Describe the three things that you are most brilliant at doing.

Describe the three things that you are weak at doing.

Look at where you are now, what opportunity can you see?

Is there a demand on you to meet a need? What is that need? Why do people come to you to meet that specific need?

Write down the things you do so easily and well.

"Do what you can with what you have where you are."
- Theodore Roosevelt

Chapter 2

Your Natural Drive: The Law Of Passion Passion Will Keep You Going

A key ingredient in fulfilling your destiny is passion. No great things are ever accomplished without it.

What is passion? Is it merely excitement or zeal? The word passion originally meant a suffering, especially that of Jesus Christ. Millions of people have seen Mel Gibson's motion picture, "The Passion of the Christ," in which the agony of Jesus is graphically displayed. Through his extreme, passionate suffering, Jesus reconciled sinners with God.

Passion is the word we use also to mean any strong, intense feeling or drive to do something. Of course, there is also the passion of romantic love. Often when we hear of a troubled marriage, we hear someone explain that "the passion is gone" from the relationship. If a couple can sustain a strong and passionate love, they can weather the many storms of life, but if there is no passion, they feel as if they are living in a cold house where the fire no longer burns in the fireplace.

A person who has talent but no passion will find it very difficult to succeed. The world is full of talented people who have not discovered their destiny, or they have not pursued it with passion. Passion is a fire that you have for something. It is a force that infuses your life with meaning, joy, and fosters commitment and determination. When passion is guided by wrong motives, it can be dangerous. Everybody does not have passion for everything; that is why you have to know where your passion lies.

I remember very well going to a church and listening to a pastor friend of mine preach. He is a powerful preacher, and his series of sermons were educational. Many people lined up to buy his tapes after the service. "Pastor, are you considering writing books?" I asked him. He gave me a funny look. "Kwame, I do not have a passion for it," he explained. Even Billy Graham, the greatest evangelistic preacher in the world, apparently never had a passion for becoming a local pastor of a church. He knew what he was called to do and what he did not have the fire to do.

Tommy Tyson, the first Chaplain of Oral Roberts University, described passion as the one thing you love doing so much, instead of demanding to be paid for it, you would gladly pay others to allow you to do it if you could. He described people who so enjoyed their work, they would do it without any pay if it were possible. How many people can say that about their work today?

We were made in the image of God who honors us with passion so we can do the things that he has assigned us to do. Allow me to ask you these questions:

- Are you doing the things you are really good at?
- Are you really thankful for what you are doing right now?
- Does the cause for which you are fighting go beyond making money?
- Does what you are doing create meaning in your life?

If your answer to these questions is yes, then you are truly blessed with a passion that will take you beyond any limitation and opposition in your path. Allow me to share with you what passion does in your life.

1. PASSION WILL MOVE YOU TO RADICAL ACTION

> Neh 1:1-4 [1]THE WORDS or story of Nehemiah son of Hacaliah: Now in the month of Chislev in the twentieth year [of the Persian king], as I was in the castle of Shushan,
>
> [2]Hanani, one of my kinsmen, came with certain men from Judah, and I asked them about the surviving Jews who had escaped exile, and about Jerusalem.
>
> [3]And they said to me, The remnant there in the province who escaped exile are in great trouble and reproach; the wall of Jerusalem is broken down, and its [fortified] gates are destroyed by fire.
>
> [4]When I heard this, I sat down and wept and mourned for days and fasted and prayed [constantly] before the God of heaven,

Nehemiah was standing when he heard that the walls of Jerusalem had fallen down. But he sat down and wept when he heard the news. Now that is passion: strong, intense feeling and desire for his people in distress. Remember that Nehemiah was not a priest. It was not his job to worry about the walls of Jerusalem. He was not the king of his nation. What could make a man worry so much about the walls in his country that he would cry for days? That has to do with passion.

Let me ask you: what do you cry over, what grieves you the most? What really moves you into action? Jesus was so moved with passion for his father's house that he made a whip of cords and drove all of the salesmen out of the temple. His actions reminded his disciples of the words from Psalm 69:9 "Zeal for thy house has consumed me" (John 2:13-17).

I heard about a man whose daughter was hit by a passing car and she was dragged under the vehicle. When her father got to the scene, he took a deep breath, grabbed hold of the car, and lifted the car from off his daughter. Everybody was shocked at what this man did. The love that he had for his daughter caused a great amount of energy to flow from within him. That is what we are talking about--the kind of love that you have for something.

2. NO ONE CAN TALK YOU OUT OF PASSION

I once heard Bishop T.D. Jakes tell his audience that he does not encourage his children to go into the ministry merely because it is his life's work. He wants them to hear that call for themselves. He explained that if his children are really called of God, no one could talk them out of it.

If I had no passion for the ministry, I would have been talked out of it long ago. In 1994, I started a church in Holland that grew to a congregation of 100, only to see it fall apart until there was not one person remaining. When a pastor loses his entire church, that would seem like a good time for him to simply give up on the ministry.

Shortly after I arrived in America in October of 1995, I started a prayer meeting in one of the houses of a Christian brother. After the meeting, I had to take one of the ladies home, and being an inexperienced driver, I ran into another car. To make matters worse, the car I was driving was not mine; the owner had loaned the keys to a friend of mine with instructions to take care of the car until she returned. The damage to the car

I was driving cost me $2000.00, and the other car cost me $5000.00. I paid for that mistake for many years.

In addition to these trials, I have endured false accusations and great financial difficulty that has affected my family. I once took all my books to the pawnshop just to get some money. For a time after moving to North Carolina, my family and I had to sleep in a pastor's office. I remember one particular night the whole family slept in my car because there was no place to lay our heads. But even through these trials, God's passion has sustained me and kept me moving forward.

Passion is what separates the great entrepreneur from others who only dream about success. Passion drives the athlete to return to the game when his muscles must be screaming for a break. Passion for life keeps prisoners of war alive and able to endure mistreatment. Passion kept Thomas Edison on task after he had failed more than one hundred times in his quest to invent the light bulb.

We hear much discussion about how hard it is to focus; there are too many distractions in today's world. But passion will intensify your focus. I have seen professors and ministers who are so focused on communicating their ideas that a train could have come roaring through the room and not upset their concentration.

Passionate workers do quality work. The cure for poor quality and laziness in the workplace is passion. When workers are excited by their work, they will strive for excellence and not be satisfied with less than perfect. A passionate person has a higher internal standard than a bored person who is merely trying to mark time.

Passion is also the way to defeat our worst enemy: fear. We fear what others might think if we fail; we fear a loss of security; and some people even fear success. But when the passion of the Lord burns within you, it consumes all fear.

If you have passion, you do not care what others think or how you might appear to the world. Be bold in pursuing your destiny with the gift of passion.

ACTION ITEM

Read the story of Noah and the flood (Genesis 6-8). How do you think this very old man looked to his neighbors as he was building a huge boat on dry ground before the flood? They must have thought he was crazy. Yet Noah remained focused on the task before him, passionately building the ark to the exact standards God gave him. Passion does not take a poll to determine what others think; it simply acts. When the rains fell and the floodwaters raged, Noah and his family were safe in the ark.

QUESTIONS TO PONDER:

What has been the driving force of my life?

What am I excited about in my life?

What am I grateful about in my life?

What am I enjoying the most in my life?

"What lies behind us and...
lies before us are tiny matters compared to...
What lies within us."
-Oliver Wendell Homes

Chapter 3

YOUR NATURAL KNOWING "A BUILT-IN KNOWLEDGE" IN YOUR HEART

You are most intuitive in the area of your calling and destiny, and that is the blessing of God. For example, a pastor is more intuitive in the pastoral field than in evangelism. In the same way, an evangelist is more intuitive in the area of evangelism than in the pastoral field.

There is a knowledge that comes naturally from within you; it is a kind of knowledge that is connected to your purpose. A practical example is how Adam knew his wife.

Genesis 2:23: "And Adam said this is now bone of my bones, and flesh of my flesh, she shall be called woman because she was taking out of man."

From this quotation we see that when God brought Eve to Adam, He did not tell Adam where Eve came from. God just kept quiet, but Adam himself knew from within that Eve was someone or something that was part of him. Allow me to share with you how the built-in knowledge within Adam helped him to recognize his future wife after he had made several attempts without any results.

1. Built-In Knowledge Helped Him Overcome Past Struggles

First and foremost, Adam said, "This is now." (Genesis 2:23). Notice the word "NOW." It was like someone who has been searching for some answers in his life and when finally he finds it, with great excitement he shouts with joy. That is exactly what Adam did. Somehow he is saying, "This is what I have been searching for!" Something within him connected to Eve and all of a sudden he knew that she was his wife. The animals could not provide Adam with fellowship or help him fulfill his destiny. Adam tried to find a friend among the animals but he found none. The moment Eve was introduced to him, Adam knew for sure that this is the one that God had brought to him to be his companion. You may ask, "How did he know this?" Adam knew because Eve was part of him. There was a connection within which led him to have inside information without God saying anything to him. Once you find something that you were destined for, your ability to relate to it is always stronger.

I believe that we often struggle because we fail to humble ourselves to follow the green light from within us. Adam became frustrated after many struggles of searching for his life partner. Just like anything he probably felt discouraged. Does it sound familiar? A lady walked up to me after I had finished preaching in London. She asked me to pray for her future partner and I prayed for her but then I asked her, "How would you know that the one that you meet is your life partner?" Of course, hearing me teaching along this line, she said "I would know it from within." In other words, if the person was really from God, she will hear it from her inside knowledge. The second thing that happened to Adam by the help of his built in knowledge was......

2. He Knew What He Was Divinely Connected To

Adam knew Eve was his wife. "This is now the bone of my bones and the flesh of my flesh." Adam used the word "my" two times in this verse. What does that mean? It means that by the help of his inside knowing, he knew that he knew who Eve was. You will always know for sure and have peace in your heart if you settle for your destiny. Have you ever experienced something that you knew without the ability to prove why? Our spiritual senses are more awake in the area that God has put us to function in. Look at the significance of what he said: "The bone of my bone and the flesh of my flesh" speaks of knowing the very core of God's will; the bone could mean the structure or foundation upon which something stands. Adam passed on beyond the physical body of Eve and talked about her bone. Whenever a person listens to his or her heart in the direction that God wants you to go, you would not worry about the physical aspect of something, you would go beyond the surface. The third thing that happened to him was....

3. He Had A Sense Of Creativity

He prophesied "And Adam called his wife Eve because she was the mother of living" (Genesis 3:20). Adam senses in his spirit that he could now continue creation as God had said through Eve. "And God blessed them and God said unto them, be fruitful and multiply and replenish the earth and subdue it and have dominion over the fish of the sea and over the fowl of the air and over every living thing that move over the earth" (Genesis 1:28).

This was the plan of God for Adam, the ability to continue creation. God made us in his image, and so we are created with creativity. This gift, however, could be more evident only when you connect it to your purpose. Whenever you take an artist into an empty room, often he will begin to talk about what needs to be done and all the designs that are necessary to bring the room to the next level. Creativity is important to your destiny. It helps you to see where you are going before you get there, and even in the midst of adversity you can still see your way. All these blessings are already built in your heart. Stay with me as we share more about your heart and destiny.

"Trust in the Lord with all thine heart; and lean not unto thine own understanding. In all thy ways acknowledge Him, and He shall direct thy paths." (Proverbs 3:5-6)

God speaks to us through our spirit. Our spirit is like a candle or a light that God has placed deep inside us. The Bible says that "The spirit of man is the candle of the Lord" (Proverbs 20:27). If we would only listen to our hearts and see our lives in the light of God's love, we would see clearly the plans he has for us. Those plans often require some struggle before we see them come to pass. Your heart can communicate to you in several ways; it could be in the form of a message or it could also come to you as a thought or a voice. Sometimes it is just a sense of a knowing within you. An indicator that the message is in line with God's plan for your life is the sense of joy, clarity, the feeling of greatness, passion and excitement in you.

GOD HAS THE ANSWERS YOU NEED INSIDE YOU

Often we try to get all our help from the outside of us at the expense of the deposit that God has already made in us. The

Bible teaches us to ask and we shall receive, but I want to tell you that sometimes the answers we need come from within by God.

One of the greatest miracles I have ever experienced came as a result of following my heart. My family and I moved from Virginia to North Carolina exactly two weeks after the terrorist attacks of September 11, 2001. I did not have a job, and we were trusting God to meet all of our needs. One day I saw a sign on Capital Boulevard in Raleigh that read, *"Follow Your Heart and You Will See Where It Will Lead You."* I recognized this as based on a biblical truth, but the idea seemed to strike me as if I had never heard it before. I had followed my heart to Raleigh without a job, and with a family of four. We were struggling, and soon God blessed us with one more child, Edna.

A wonderful woman of God opened her home to us for three months. I will always appreciate her kindness. At the end of the three months, I did not know where to move my family because we did not have enough money to rent a house or an apartment. One night in a dream I saw that we must leave this woman's house, even if we had no place to go. I woke up from my sleep with a strong urgency in my heart to get out. "But where are we going?" my wife asked me. "I don't know yet, but let's start packing," I replied. And so, in the middle of the night, we packed up all our earthly possessions.

As I was packing, I thought of a friend to call who could help us. He took us to a hotel and paid for our stay there for a month. While we were there, my children began to complain: "Daddy, why can't we eat yogurt? Why can't we have our own house? Why don't we have our own furniture?" My wife made a soup with only chicken wings for flavor. It was simple and delicious to us because we were hungry.

Our stay at the hotel ended, but our financial struggle continued. Another couple allowed us to stay in their home for a couple of days. Again, I woke up with the urgency in my heart that we should keep moving and not remain long in this place, lest our generous friends become concerned that we might take advantage of their hospitality. This time, we moved to a pastor's office where we slept for several nights before the Lord provided us with our own apartment.

One day as I passed by a particular church, I pointed at the building and said to my wife, "One day, I am going to visit that church." Several weeks later, I went there. After the service, a man and his wife introduced themselves to me. "I am David, and this my wife Dawn," the man said. "God informed us through a prophetic word that he was going to send a couple our way in the second week of January. You came here at the exact time the Lord said you would come."

While I had been in the midst of a time of severe testing, God had already prepared this couple to meet my family and to help us get established. They bought a townhouse for us and told us to stay there for an entire year without any payment. Now that is a miracle in America!

Follow your heart, and it will lead you to a wealthy place, a place of blessings. As a child of God, your job is to follow God through his word: "Thy word is a lamp unto my feet, and a light unto my path" (Psalms 119:105).

I read some time ago, that the human spirit is limitless. In other words, you are not limited in the things you can do. Somebody has said that there are two kinds of worlds, the inner world and the outer world. The outer world is where we see and experience all the things that we go through. The inner world is your heart where God has deposited great and awesome treasures.

THREE THINGS TO KNOW AS YOU LEARN TO FOLLOW YOUR HEART

1) Stop Being Negative

Proverbs 23:7 "For as he thicket in his heart, so is he: Eat and drink, saith he to thee; but his heart is not with thee."

This is the reason why you should not entertain negative thoughts in your head because it can affect your destiny. The devil will constantly throw evil thoughts in your minds just so you will begin to accept it and go with it.

2) Choose to Listen to Inspired Conversation

God will use conversations to inspire you. Have you ever joined a conversation where the people are talking about a subject that interests you, and all of a sudden something inside of you jumps up and you feel so great just listening to that conversation because you are getting inspired. If a conversation strikes you to the point that you want to join the people who are talking, it is a clue to what God wants to do in your life.

3) Read About People Who Have Been Where You Are Going

People who have achieved in spite of extreme adversity.

I watched a movie about a guy who was born with a strong speech impediment. In addition to that he had a physical disability that made it impossible for him to get dressed without assistance. He could not complete his education because the kids would laugh at him. He had to stop school and stay home with his mom. One of the things that his mom told him was that no matter your circumstance if you believe that you can make a difference, then nothing can stop you. I will call him Bob. So, Bob believed the saying of his mother and by that he closed his eyes to all those negative thoughts that could stop him from fulfilling his God-given destiny. One day his mother got so sick that she died, leaving Bob to face the world alone. Well, Bob grew up with no skill and no educational background. He put in many applications for a job, but because of his speech, no one would hire him.

He did not give up but held on to his mom's saying, "If you can believe, you can make it." Bob heard of a company that sells cosmetics door-to-door. He applied for the job and got rejected on several occasions. The company thought that their business was all about communication, and they believed Bob could not speak clearly enough to explain the products to the customers. Bob did not give up. The only other choice he had was to give up and either find a shelter or become homeless. Sitting there and watching the movie, I cried from this point until the end. It was very moving. One day Bob dressed up by the help of his friend and went to the same company and got hired.

His next challenge was how to go to the houses and talk to them about the product. In all, about twenty four houses rejected him because once he knocked on the door and someone answered, they would realize that he was not making sense. On one occasion, the kids hit him while closing the door. As he kept on trying, one day a woman opened the door for him, not just for the sake of the product, but she was moved by his physical disabilities. Bob was very friendly. He loved children, and he sat there playing with the kids. It touched the woman so much that she bought some merchandise. Bob came home that day very happy, and since he could not use both hands to type, he used one hand to type the invoice for the woman. In all, it took him one hour just to type her name and address.

Pretty soon people in the community heard of him and started inviting him to sell, Bob ended up hiring people and now he is a millionaire in America.

ACTION ITEM

The Bible often refers to the heart as being the deepest part of us. Our hearts can lead us toward God or away from him. A pure heart is inclined toward a close relationship with our Creator.

Make these words your prayer today:

"Create in me a clean heart, O God; and renew a right spirit within me."

Psalm 51:10

QUESTIONS TO PONDER:

Write ten things you do that make you feel being yourself.

Write a list of things that you are more creative doing.

"Success is a ladder that be climbed with your hands in your pockets. Do something."

—American proverb

Chapter 4

GET CONNECTED TO YOUR SOURCE

Are you linked to the world, but disconnected from God?

Our world is linked and connected as never before. Many of us use communications technology, such as cell phones, daily. Distances between nations and peoples vanish in seconds as we send email around the world from our homes and offices and from mobile devices we carry everywhere. Information that used to take hours or days to reach the masses is now available in real time. Billions of viewers from many nations witness events as they happen: a royal wedding in Spain, a tornado in Oklahoma, the fall of a dictator's statue in Iraq.

The children born in the 1960s saw humans visit the moon; children born today will probably witness colonies on the moon, humans landing on Mars, and amazing new cures for old illnesses that have plagued mankind throughout history. The next twenty-five years of our lives promise to bring enormous and rapid changes in science, technology, energy, culture, and commerce. Every day people are breaking records, running faster, jumping higher, and making more money that we previously thought possible.

How could it be that, in the midst of amazing progress, many people are unhappy, struggling to survive from one day to the next? Perhaps you are one of these people, or you know someone who is in this category. These are the hardworking people who drag themselves out of bed in the morning, wondering how they can make it through another day of work, traffic, bills to pay, children to raise, meals to prepare, and conflicts to resolve. Most of us have been tempted to cure our frustration by resigning ourselves to our fate. "This is just the way it is," we tell ourselves, "my life will never change."

Theologians and philosophers have wrestled with questions about the meaning of life for centuries. Technology cannot erase the fact that we are spiritual beings with needs far beyond the physical requirements our bodies need to survive. We need more than faster cars, big-screen televisions, computers, and fancy clothes. An overflow of information, instead of uplifting our spirits, can distract us from what matters the most: discovering who we really are and what God wants us to do in the years we have on this earth. None of us wants to look back on our lives with regret, having missed our calling by spending years spinning our wheels, struggling with tasks not suited to us, merely to afford the gadgets and lifestyles our society says we must have.

Get connected to our Source so we may know how to express and exercise our gifts.

In today's world with innumerable competing voices demanding our attention, making time for our Creator is crucial to staying focused on who we really are. The demands of modern life require us to juggle several activities as once, to multitask. Businesses value employees who can handle several tasks simultaneously. Sometimes this idea is carried to a comical extreme. I once saw an employee at her desk, carrying on two conversations, one on a cell phone and one on the phone at her desk, while she typed a response to an email on her computer and listened to the radio.

In Genesis, we read that Adam and Eve "heard the voice of the Lord God walking in the cool of the day" (Gen 3:8). They did not hear God shouting over the sound of the winds or over the roar of wild animals. God spoke in the cool of the day, not in the heat of the afternoon or in the midst of the first couple's work of caring for the Garden. Even in the most ideal setting of all time, the Garden of Eden, God had a special time to commune with his creation. None of us lives in an ideal world today; therefore, it is even more important for us to make time with one who knows us best.

When Jesus prayed, He gave God his full attention.

When Jesus taught his disciples and followers, He did not scream over the noisy crowds in order to get to his point across. The Gospel writers tell us people often came to Jesus to ask questions of him because he was a respected teacher and healer. Jesus explained the requirement of being born again to Nicodemus, a ruler who came at night to speak with him (John 3:1-21). Physically sick people sought Jesus wherever he went, hoping to touch even the edge of his garment so they might be healed (Mark 6:56). It is interesting how Matthew reports friends and relatives of those possessed with demons brought the afflicted to Jesus "When the evening was come" (Matthew 8:16) Perhaps it was simply more convenient to bring these people to Jesus after the working day was done; however, I believe Jesus set aside a special time for dealing with certain groups of the sick and afflicted.

Jesus knew that to get connected to his source, his heavenly father, he had to disconnect from other distractions. Even the Son of God needed special times and places to focus on his mission. Once when the multitudes became too great, he got in a boat and left the crowd (Matthew 8:18-23). Modern business consultants tell us to "maximize" our opportunities and always follow up on potential customers. Yet Jesus left when the crowd became huge, and he sailed right into a storm. When the disciples panicked, Jesus chastised them for their lack of faith and calmed the winds and the sea (Matthew 8:24-27). Imagine how some "experts" today would criticize Jesus for his poor marketing, lack of planning, and failure to consult the weather report before risking lives in the boat. Jesus consulted his father in prayer and acted according to what he knew his father wanted him to do, not what a thousand other voices were telling him to do.

When we read of Jesus communicating with God, it is usually on a mountainside (Mark 6:46, Luke 6:12), a garden (Mark 14:33), a desert place (Luke 9:10), or, as in one report, "a solitary place" (Mark 1:35). All of the Gospel writers believed it was important to record the time and place of many of Jesus' prayers. Of course God can speak to us at any time and in any manner he chooses, but he knows we humans have an attention problem when it comes to hearing his still, small voice. If we are preoccupied with television, movies, video games, and stock market reports, we cannot expect God to shout over all the chatter to teach us what we need to know about our lives. In the life of Jesus, we see a man who took prayer seriously and dedicated a time and a place for it. In our fast-moving world, it is crucial for us to learn from our Savior's example because if we do not make an effort to commune with the eternal, then the temporal things will surely devour all of our time.

Television can be a good tool for education, but it can also be a great distraction.

We hear many arguments about whether organized prayer should be allowed in public schools. It is sad to say that while many of us are concerned about prayer in schools, we have no time for God in our homes. Which creates more of a crisis in your home: losing your Bible or losing the remote control to your television? Some of the worst family struggles are over who lost the remote control. Parents demand that all activity cease until the family can find it, demonstrating to the children that television is the most important thing in their lives. Many families have televisions in almost every room in the house, making it impossible to read, study, or meditate. People wonder why they are so stressed and where their time goes. Sadly, for many people, their time and lives are consumed by television as an increasing number of channels flows into our homes. I know of one father who became so frustrated with his children's wasting time on cable television that he cancelled his cable subscription. All that remained were approximately three of four fuzzy channels. Unfortunately, his children still did not use their time wisely. They continued to watch whatever programs were on. They were accustomed to the television as a friend and babysitter. If we do not reclaim our time, the television will take our time from us because it is always ready. I want us to take the same passion we have for television and apply it to getting a vision from God. Then, we can say that television has become "tell vision" because we will emerge from our time with God with a new understanding that was not possible when we were feeding ourselves on whatever programs came out of the television set. I am not laying down a law requiring those who seek God to throw away their televisions. I have my own television ministry that reaches people from all walks of life. I am, however, asking you to do an inventory of the number of hours your family spend on television. Is the television always on in your house, from the time you come home from work until you go to bed at night? That amounts to approximately six hours of television per day, forty-two hours per week, eighty-eight hours per month, and more than one thousand hours per year. Think of what you could do with one thousand extra hours in your schedule! Ask yourself if perhaps some of your depression and confusion could be directly related to the amount of time you are not spending with God because you are allowing an extreme amount of television and other diversions to run your life.

Connect with your divine surroundings.

We humans are perfectly suited to living on God's beautiful earth. The water, air, and other natural resources we need to survive are all here. As far as we know, no other planets in our galaxy can sustain human life.

Some environments are life-giving and sustaining, while others drag us down and block the flow of our life and gifts. A fish's naturally divine environment is in water, where it can swim with lightning speed, reproduce, and travel in schools with countless other fish. If we take that same beautiful, elegant, and fast-moving fish out of the water and put it on land, it can do nothing. If the fish remains on land, it is soon not even fit for a scavenger to eat.

An eagle in the sky is the king of all birds, soaring and navigating its path across the skies. That same magnificent eagle would not live long in the ocean. The fish and the eagle need the right environment to fulfill their purpose. With a supportive environment, these are wonderful creatures. It is sad to even think of what happens to animals in the wrong environment. Thank God that we humans have the power to change our surroundings and our thinking.

Certain places light a fire in my spirit. When I drive through the rolling, green hills of the Shenandoah Valley in Virginia, or gaze out upon the ocean as the sea gulls dive into the water to catch fish, my spirit soars. I have a similar uplifting experience when I take a prayer walk, prepare a lesson on finding our potential, or teach a group of receptive believers. These environments draw the gift out of me, making me feel physically lighter and faster. On the other hand, some surroundings make me feel put down and unable to do anything.

The distance between where you are now and where you are going is the people around you.

Our associations with others will help us to succeed or fail.

Jesus could not do many miracles in his own hometown because of the unbelief and negativity of the people there. When he spoke in the local synagogue, the crowd did not receive Jesus' saying as good news. Instead, they were offended by this hometown boy who thought he was something special:

> "Is not this the carpenter's son? Is not his mother called Mary?
> And his brethren, James, and Joseph, and Simon, and Judas? And his
> sisters, are they not all with us? From where, then, hath this man all
> these things? And they were offended in him. But Jesus said unto them, 'A
> prophet is not without honor, except in his own country, and in his own house.'
> And he did not many mighty works there because of their unbelief."
>
> Matthew 13:55-58.

If Jesus had to make changes in his surroundings and associations in order to allow God's power to flow through him, we must also be ready to make necessary changes. I cannot tell you what specific changes you need to make in your life. Only you know that. Perhaps you need to move from where you have been living in order to make a new start. You may have to relocate to get a better job. It could be time to stop hanging around people who bring you down and start spending time with people who build you up and cause you to think higher thoughts. Eve messed up the most beautiful place on earth, the Garden of Eden, by her association with the serpent (Genesis 3). The mighty Sampson died far too young because he surrounded himself with the wicked Delilah (Judges 16).

Good friends will challenge you to stir up the gift inside you; they will encourage you to stretch your boundaries. Proverbs

13:20 says, "He that walketh with wise men shall be wise, but a companion of fools shall be destroyed."

You can gain insight into your destiny through prayers.

I like to take a prayer walk early in the morning in order to get connected to my source. I leave the house before the bad news of the day can reach me through a television or radio, before anything else can absorb this special time. Although I live in a city and not on a mountain or in the desert, I still gain inner strength from walking and praying, even as cars speed past me. My wife says she is worried someone will call the police and report a strange man walking around talking to himself. But I am not talking to myself. I talk to my love, my Jesus, and to my heavenly daddy. I pray for guidance for the day, for the needs of my city and church, and my family.

I also have a prayer closet in my home where I spend ten to twenty minutes each day. Most of the time God speaks to me as I am coming out of my prayer closet. It takes time to forget the cares of this life and its details, but after I have done that, my spirit is receptive to his leading. I usually emerge from prayer with some ideas, and as I act on those ideas, I begin to see miracles happening immediately. For example, one day, as I left my prayer closet, the Lord told me, "A lady is coming to visit you. Pray that she will give you a donation for your television ministry." I asked God, "How about one hundred dollars?" This lady soon arrived with a check for one hundred dollars. I had received this idea in my prayer closet.

On another occasion, I had been praying for several hours. I was in financial need, but I did not want to call anyone and ask for money. As I was finishing my prayer time, the Lord spoke softly to my spirit, "Someone is coming with three hundred dollars." Less than two hours later, someone arrived with three hundred dollars. I did not have to call anyone. I have seen God move many times in this way. I cannot live without my prayer. God is going to bless you if you retain a quality prayer time with him.

Jesus is saying to you, "Behold, I stand at the door and knock; if any man hear my voice, and open the door, I will come in to him, and will sup with him, and he with me" (Rev. 3:20). This verse is not for evangelism. It is not primarily a call to unbelievers. This is Jesus calling for fellowship with believers who have left him homeless because they are too busy to open their doors to him. Have you ever felt like someone you loved has shut the door on you? You want to communicate with the person, but he or she is emotionally unavailable to you. It seems your loved one has time for everything and everybody but you. The first sign of a troubled marriage is a lack of good communication. A friendship with no communication is not much of a friendship. A major reason many people have lost sight of their destiny is a broken relationship with God. The good news is you can turn this situation around immediately by getting connected to your source. Having good quality time helps you stay tune to your purpose.

The power of quality quite time

Give to God your best strength and time, he would in turn give you his best ideas and thoughts concerning your life. On a daily basis you need to make time to seek the Lord by way of prayer, meditation, reading or being still in his presence. God rewards us for seeking him. "I love them that love me and those that seek me early shall find me" (Proverbs 8:17).

"But without faith it is impossible to please God for he that comes to God must believe that He is and that He is a rewarder of them that diligently seek Him" (Hebrews 11:6)

"Call unto me and I will answer thee and show thee great and mighty things which thou knowest not" (Jeremiah 33:3)

What to look for during and after your quite time with God

Watch words from God that seems to hit you, registers on your heart, moves you, touches you and stay with you. God's word often moves our hearts if we are humble in his presence.

Watch activities around you, God may be speaking through your circumstance. God may be telling you what He is about to do or is doing in your life at the present moment.

Follow His plans as He makes it known. Don't go ahead of what you know.

Psalm 119: 105 "Thy word is a lamp unto my feet and a light unto my path"

Sometimes God's Word is a lamp that gives us enough light to move few steps but other times, His Word is like a light to show us what could happen in the future. God calls people to follow Him by faith. He does not always reveal everything at one time. In some cases, God gave more details than in others. Like in the case of Abram, it was very little information.

"Now the Lord had said to Abram, get thee out of thy country and from thy kindred and from thy fathers house unto a land that I will show thee" Genesis 12:1. For Peter, Andrew, James, John (Matthew 4:18-20, 21-22), Matthew (Matthew 9:9), and Paul (Acts 9:1-20) God gave very little detail about their assignment.

Watch what God is doing, where He is working and join Him

John 5:19-20 "Then answered Jesus and said unto them, Verily, verily, I say unto you, The Son can do nothing of himself, but what he seeth the Father do: for what things soever He doeth, these also doeth the Son likewise. For the Father loveth the Son, and sheweth him all things that Himself doeth: and He will shew him greater works than these, that ye may marvel." Jesus was never frustrated about the plans of God, He got involved in His father's business as the father reveals to Him.

A certain pastor and his staff felt led of God to start outreach ministry to the college campus. After they had tried to get it started, it never seemed to work out. The senior pastor then decided to watch and see what God is doing and join Him. He told the few students in his church to take one week to go to campus and see what God is doing. One Wednesday night one of the students reported to the pastor. She said "A friend of mine invited me to go to lunch with her and during conversation, she asked me if I know anyone who can lead them in Bible studies, eleven girls had been meeting in her dorm and they needed a leader." Three Bible studies class got started as a result of watching and joining what God was doing. God used the same principles to bring victory to Israel through Gideon.

Judges 7:9-11 "And it came to pass the same night, that the LORD said unto him, Arise, get thee down unto the host; for I have delivered it into thine hand. But if thou fear to go down, go thou with Phurah thy servant down to the host, And thou shalt hear what they say....."

God wanted to destroy the Midianites through Gideon but because he was afraid to go down to the camp of the Midianites, God told him to go to the camp by night and there, he heard of two people talking. One of them had seen a dream of a sword and the other interpreted it as the sword of Gideon. When Gideon heard that, he saw what God had planned to do and that caused him to join God in the battle.

Be ready to make some adjustments

In joining God in what He is doing, you may make some adjustments. It may relate to your thinking, circumstance, relationship, commitments, actions and beliefs. Hear from God and follow Him. John 5:30

Circumstance and God's Leading

In following the plan of God, don't get in a hurry. Don't get lazy by doing nothing. Don't get discouraged. Don't make hasty conclusions in situations as failures. Don't allow your circumstance to preach to you about God. Don't allow the circumstance to interpret the word of God to you.

What you should do in circumstances

Learn to surrender to God. Be completely humble that means you surrender your will to God and be in a state where you are ready to follow His will. Let the Holy Ghost preach to you about the circumstance. Ask God His perspective in the circumstance.

Get clarity and confirmation from your family, friends and church

Sometimes God may reveal your destiny to your love ones. Following those revelations can help you improve and excel. The revelation that Peter received from God concerning Jesus Christ became a foundation for Jesus' ministry. You should however be certain that what loved ones are saying is true of you. The disciples heard a lot of opinions about and when they pointed out to Him, Jesus did not make any comments. Why? He knew which opinion was in line with the Word of God concerning Him. Peter said, Thou are the Christ the Son of the Living God (Matthew 16:16).

Some signs that you are not in the will of God

Doing things out of God's will often result in the following: you get burn out, accomplish very little, waste God's resource, get frustrated, become bitter and lose touch with the anointing of God . Haggai 1:6-9Ye have sown much and bring in little but ye eat but ye have not enough ye drink but ye are not filled with drink ye clothe you but there is none warm and he that earn wages to put it into a bag with holes, ye looked for much and lo it came too little and when ye brought it home I did blow upon it......."

ACTION ITEM:

Begin a daily prayer walk or establish your prayer closet where you will not be interrupted by others or by any electronic media such as televisions or cell phones. Pray to God in your own words, thanking Him for His blessings, and let Him know your requests. You can be yourself with God. Start your special time and place of communion with Him today.

Unleash the talents within you. Overcome those areas in your life that you feel are "handicaps." Succeed despite those things that would hold you back.

Chapter 5

DISCOVERING YOUR SPIRITUAL GIFTS

One question that I hear frequently is: "How do you discover your spiritual gifts?" A lot of people want to know but they do not know how. Still others, who know their gifts fail to use them. Many of us are also ignorant of how many gifts are at our disposal. We limit ourselves by the very few gifts that we see in our churches so that we do not even think that what we have are also spiritual gifts. There is a difference between natural gifts (talent) and spiritual gifts. Natural gifts are given to you from natural birth; spiritual gifts are given to you from your spiritual birth. Natural gifts are used for the benefits of the people who possess the gifts; spiritual gifts, however, are used for the benefits of others. There are some natural gifts that God can anoint and use as a spiritual gift.

Each gift has its own way or style of operation
I Corinthians 12:4-6

[4]Now there are diversities of gifts, but the same Spirit. [5]And there are differences of administrations, but the same Lord. [6]And there are diversities of operations, but it is the same God which worketh all in all.

This means that if, for example, you compare two people who exercise the gift of teaching, and someone could be used of God to teach one topic, while another who is also a teacher could teach anything. Four people who have the same gift can use it differently. There are many kinds of spiritual gifts. Let us explore some of them

A. *GIFTS THAT ARE GIFTS AND MANISFESTATIONS* *1 Corinthians 12*

Three revelation gifts--these gifts reveal something

- ✓ The word of wisdom
- ✓ The word of knowledge
- ✓ The discerning of spirits

Three power gifts--these gifts do something

- ✓ The gift of faith
- ✓ The working of miracles
- ✓ The gifts of healings

Three utterance gifts--these gifts say something

- ✓ Prophecy
- ✓ Diverse kinds of tongues
- ✓ Interpretation of tongues

B. THE GIFT OF ADMINISTRATION
Ephesians 4:11-13

11And he gave some, apostles; and some, prophets; and
some, evangelists; and some, pastors and teachers; 12For the
perfecting of the saints, for the work of the ministry, for the
edifying of the body of Christ: 13Till we all come in the unity
of the faith, and of the knowledge of the Son of God, unto a
perfect man, unto the measure of the stature of the fullness
of Christ.

C. CONGREGATIONAL GIFTS
Romans 12 :27-31

27Now ye are the body of Christ, and members in
particular. 28And God hath set some in the church, first
apostles, secondarily prophets, thirdly teachers, after
that miracles, then gifts of healings, helps, governments,
diversities of tongues. 29*Are* all apostles? *are* all prophets? *are*
all teachers? *are* all workers of miracles? 30Have all the gifts
of healing? do all speak with tongues? do all interpret? 31But
covet earnestly the best gifts: and yet show I unto you a more
excellent way.

And

Romans 12:3-8

For I say, through the grace given unto me, to every man that is among you, not to think *of himself* more highly than he ought to think; but to think soberly, according as God hath dealt to every man the measure of faith. [4]For as we have many members in one body, and all members have not the same office: [5]So we, *being* many, are one body in Christ, and every one members one of another. [6]Having then gifts differing according to the grace that is given to us, whether prophecy, *let us prophesy* according to the proportion of faith; [7]Or ministry, *let us wait* on *our* ministering: or he that teacheth, on teaching; [8]Or he that exhorteth, on exhortation: he that giveth, *let him do it* with simplicity; he that ruleth, with diligence; he that showeth mercy, with cheerfulness.

There are so many spiritual gifts available to us. No one can say, "I do not have anything to do," or "I am not important." There are several gifts that the Bible describes as plural, meaning we have different kinds of such gifts.

Also each gift that you take can be varied in operation, style, administration, and uses.

D. MORE ADDITIONAL GIFTS
GIFTS THAT DEMONSTRATE GOD'S LOVE
SERVICE Acts 6:1-7

The ability to recognize unmet needs in the church family, and take the initiative to provide practical assistance quickly, cheerfully, and without a need for recognition.

MERCY Luke 10:30-37

The ability to detect hurt and empathize with those who are suffering in the church family. The ability to provide compassionate and cheerful support to those experiencing distress, crisis, or pain.

HOSPITALITY 1 Peter 4:9-10

The ability to make others, especially strangers, feel warmly welcomed, accepted, and comfortable in the church family. The ability to coordinate factors that promote fellowship.

INTERCESSION Col. 1:9-12

The ability to pray for the needs of others in the church family over extended periods of time on a regular basis. The ability to persist in prayer and not be discouraged until the answer arrives.

GIFTS THAT CELEBRATE GOD'S PRESENCE

(Worship or prayer-related gifts)

MUSIC Psalm 150

The ability to celebrate God's presence through music, either vocal or instrumental, and to lead the church family in worship.

ARTS & CRAFTS Exodus 31:3-11

The ability to build, maintain, or beautify the place of worship for God's glory. The ability to express worship through a variety of art forms. Now knowing that there are numerous of gifts available for us, let us talk about five most important facts about spiritual gifts.

Allow me to share with you five important facts about your spiritual gifts.

Fact # 1
God does not want you to be ignorant about your gifts

I Corinthians 7:12 "Now concerning spiritual *gifts*, brethren, I would not have you ignorant." God has deposited a lot of treasure in us and it is our responsibility to search it out. Our gifting and talents make us unique. The devil has a way of making you think that you have nothing to offer and once you accept that, then he will make you think that you amount to nothing. In the Garden of Eden we have an account of the devil trying to confuse Eve into thinking about an image she was not.

Genesis 3:4-5 "[4]And the serpent said unto the woman, Ye shall not surely die: [5]For God doth know that in the day ye eat thereof, then your eyes shall be opened, and ye shall be as gods, knowing good and evil."

Eve was confused and she became deceived by the image that the devil had placed before her. God created Adam and Eve in his own image and likeness (Genesis 1:26-27). Eating from the tree of knowledge of good and evil did not make them more than they were. They were rather reduced from what God had made them. They fell short of the glory of God. Before the fall they were the masterpiece of God; they were in control of the earth, and the devil had no power over them

Genesis 1:26 "[26]And God said, Let us make man in our image, after our likeness: and let them have dominion over the fish of the sea, and over the fowl of the air, and over the cattle, and over all the earth, and over every creeping thing that creepeth upon the earth."

Did you notice the word "dominion"? It speaks of power and control. In the Garden of Eden, there were all kinds of wild animals, but they were all subject to Adam and Eve.

Adam was the highlight of God's creation. It has been estimated that inventors use one tenth of one percent of their total potential brain ability. Adam was so knowledgeable. He was able to give names to all the animals that God had created. Also, Adam and Eve seemed to understand the language of animals. The glory of God was their covering. They were like king and queen. God created them with so much glory that they had the ability to talk with God face to face like a man talking to his neighbor. The problem was that they did not know the kind of power God had placed in them. They were ignorant of the "image and likeness" they were made after. Image is everything. Satan perceived that Eve was not too strong with the image with which she was made so the devil took advantage of her ignorance.

Have you ever asked the question why the devil approached them at the time where they were standing close to the tree? He used a wrong image (the tree) to detour them from what God had already made them to be. Eve had to be convinced that she was less than what God had made her. Let us read what happened to her.

Genesis 3:6 "And when the woman saw that the tree *was* good for food, and that it *was* pleasant to the eyes, and a tree to be desired to make *one* wise, she took of the fruit thereof, and did eat, and gave also unto her husband with her; and he did eat."

By looking at the tree she had a wrong perception of herself. All of a sudden the tree that was forbidden was pleasant to the eyes of Eve (a tree to make one wise). God was no longer the image of Eve but the tree. Had Eve realized her full potential and her image in God, she would not have been deceived by the devil. Now you know why God does not want you to be ignorant of his gift in your life.

Ignorance of your gift will make you live below your standard.

John 4:9-10 [9]Then saith the woman of Samaria unto him, How is it that thou, being a Jew, askest drink of me, which am a woman of Samaria? for the Jews have no dealings with the Samaritans. [10]Jesus answered and said unto her, If thou knewest the gift of God, and who it is that saith to thee, Give me to drink; thou wouldest have asked of him, and he would have given thee living water.

You probably know the story about this Samaritan woman who met Jesus on her way to draw water from the well of Jacob. Jesus began to engage her in conversation. He asked the woman to give him a drink but the woman was reluctant because of the enmity between the Jews and Samaritans. Jesus answered her that if he knew God and the gift of God, she would have asked of him something that has life (living water).

The Samaritan woman was living below her standard; she was following after other people's husbands because she did not have a good image of herself. She did not know God, neither did she know the gift of God. She was a prostitute but she had a great gift to evangelize the world. Why did she settle for prostitution? Probably, she thought that she had nothing else to offer. Talking with Jesus a while affected her image of herself and immediately she hooked herself up with her true image. What did she do? She left the basket and went evangelizing.

Fact # 2
It is a fact that God wants you to use your gift to the fullest

Luke 19:13 [13]And he called his ten servants, and delivered them ten pounds, and said unto them, Occupy till I come.

Luke 19:20-27 And another came, saying, Lord, behold, *here is* thy pound, which I have kept laid up in a napkin: [21]For I feared thee, because thou art an austere man: thou takest up that thou layedst not down, and reapest that thou didst not sow. [22]And he saith unto him, Out of thine own mouth will I judge thee, *thou* wicked servant. Thou knewest that I was an austere man, taking up that I laid not down, and reaping that I did not sow: [23]Wherefore then gavest not thou my money into the bank, that at my coming I might have required mine own with usury? [24]And he said unto them that stood by, Take from him the pound, and give *it* to him that hath ten pounds. [25](And they said unto him, Lord, he hath ten pounds.) [26]For I say unto you, That unto every one which hath shall be given; and from him that hath not, even that he hath shall be taken away from him. [27]But those mine enemies, which would not that I should reign over them, bring hither, and slay *them* before me .

Occupy till I come

This parable talks about a man traveling to a far country and he gave gifts to his servants. The first instruction that he gave to them was "occupy till I come." Why? Because an idle mind is the workshop of the devil, and when you are really busy doing what God has assigned you to do, it is very difficult for the devil to get your attention because you are already engaged. The reason our churches are not growing is that we have so many people unoccupied and very few people doing the work. When you are busy using your gifts you do not have time to look at what others are doing or not doing. Our churches are filled with jealousy and envy because people who have not discovered their gifts are occupied with looking at what others are doing with theirs.

Idleness produces spiritual wickedness and laziness.

Luke 19:22 [22]And he saith unto him, Out of thine own mouth will I judge thee, *thou* wicked servant. Thou knewest that I was an austere man, taking up that I laid not down, and reaping that I did not sow

Have you wondered why Jesus referred to this servant as wicked? I have often thought about it. I realized that if he did not commit adultery, or fraud or murder, why then should the owner describe him as wicked? It is just simple, look at where you are right now. Probably you are in your bedroom reading this book or you are sitting in the hall reading. It does not matter where you are at the moment; I just want you to realize that the environment in which you live is conducive because people like you use their gifts. Everybody answers to someone in this world and in our churches. You can make someone's life better by using your God-given talent. God wants us to live our life here to make others feel better. Secondly, God has given everything we need to make our living comfortable through our gifts. The very moment you stop using yours, you stop the flow of the beauty of the church, your home, or your community. The reason why you live is so you can declare the praises of God. If that was not the reason, you could have been dead by now. The Psalmist said "I will not die. I will live to declare the praises of our God" (Psalm 118:17).

Fact # 3
You grow spiritually and receive more anointing by using your gift.

Romans 1:11 "For I long to see you that I may impart unto you some spiritual gift to the end you may be established."

Jesus put it this way in **Matthew 5:6:** "Blessed are they which do hunger and thirst after righteousness for they shall be filled."

God fills those who are hungry and thirsty. What sense does it make to fill someone or something that is already full? There is no room for the filling and that is exactly what happens; if we will be hungry, God will fill us with great things, for he said:

" I am the Lord thy God who brought thee out of the land of Egypt, open thy mouth wide and I will fill it" (Psalm 81:10).

Can you put food in the mouth of someone whose mouth is full with something else? No, not until the person has already finished eating what he or she has in his or her mouth.

The question that people often ask me is "how then can I become hungry spiritually?" You see, whenever you eat physical food and you are really full, you are no longer hungry; the food has to be digested, and the end product enters into your blood stream. The waste product is excreted, and then the system calls for more. Without the system using up what it has, it cannot ask for more. The problem with many Christians is that they have received so many blessings and because they are not ready to give, they cannot receive more from God. Jesus took the gift from the one who was not using it and gave it to the one who used his to the fullest.

A practical example is a story that I heard from Joyce Meyer. One of her staff members had worked with Joyce Meyer for a long time. She had listened to almost every single sermon of Joyce. As time went by, the woman realized that she was no longer enjoying the sermons anymore, and she started complaining. That is because she became like a stagnant river which gathers all kinds of dirt and leaves from the trees, and because she had no way of letting go of the dirty water, she started to stink.

The woman went to God to pray and fast, and she said something like this: "Lord, I love Joyce Meyer, and I have no intentions of stopping working with her, but I am not getting blessed like I used to. What should I do?" The Lord spoke to her heart, that the problem was not with Joyce Meyer, but the problem was with her. God continued to make it plain to her that she had received so much from Joyce that she had become full, and until she gave out what she had, she would not be filled. The more we give, the more we get. Try putting your gift into practice and God will fill you more and more.

Fact # 4
Spiritual gifts are not for my benefit but for the benefit of others.

"Each one of you, as a good manager of God's different gifts, must use for the good of others, the spiritual gift he has received from God." 1 Peter 4:10 (GN)

"The Holy Spirit displays God's power through each of us as a means of helping the entire church." 1 Corinthians 12:7 (TLB)

"It was He who gave gifts to men... to build up the Body of Christ so we shall all come together to that oneness in our faith... and become mature... Then we shall no longer be children, carried by the waves and blown about by every shifting wind..." Ephesians 4:11, 13-14 (GN)

"With ordinary talent and extraordinary perseverance, all things are attainable."

—Thomas Buxton

CRITICAL QUESTIONS YOU MUST ASK YOURSELF.

Gifts Loving Spouse and Mature Friends see in You.

1. Write a list of gifts your spouse sees in you.
2. Which of these gifts does your spouse see as your dominant gifts and why?
3. How would your spouse describe you?
4. Write five ways your children describe you.
5. Name five gifts mature and trusted friends say about you.

Chapter 6

ATTITUDES THAT MAKE THINGS HAPPEN FOR YOU

Roadmap # 1
Be ready to help even when you are hurting. What you make happen for somebody else, God will make happen for you.

Ruth was a woman of much pain but she decided to help someone during her grief, and the person she helped was Naomi. And she said, "Behold, thy sister in law is gone back unto her people, and unto her gods: return thou
after thy sister in law. 16And Ruth said, Entreat me not to
leave thee, *or* to return from following after thee: for whither thou goest, I will go; and where thou lodgest, I will lodge:
thy people *shall be* my people, and thy God my God: 17Where
thou diest, will I die, and there will I be buried: the LORD do so to me, and more also, *if ought* but death part thee and
me. 18When she saw that she was steadfastly minded to go
with her, then she left speaking unto her" (Ruth 1:15-18).

This is a story about Ruth who left the city of Moab to go to Bethlehem. Naomi, her mother in-law, had lost her husband and her two sons who were married to Ruth and Orpah. Life had treated Naomi so unfairly that she decided to go back to her country. Her daughters-in-law decided to go with her but Orpah went back to her country but Ruth stayed with her mother in law.

Now Ruth cleaved to her mother-in-law. She must have thought, "Naomi came to this town empty, and now who would take care of this old woman?" A lot of things were against Ruth that could have discouraged her from helping her mother in-law. She herself was a widow, her husband was also dead: her past life was very painful. A lot of times we lose the blessings of God because we let our past pain get in the way.

Sometimes you have to help someone while you are still going through a very tough time. Several years ago, I went to a friend to help me with something we were doing in our church. He was the kind of person who could get things done. On that particular day, something was different. After we had talked about the program, he was willing to help, but all of a sudden, his countenance changed and he began to tell me of how people in the past have hurt him. I told him not to help me under pressure because I felt for him. The past can stop you from realizing your God-given destiny.

Ruth had to deal with the returning of Orpah. She was being encouraged by her sister in-law because she was also traveling with her. Sometimes our present situations do not help us to move forward to the Promised Land because our friends are causing us much pain. Jesus sent his disciples two by two so that if one is weak, the other could support him, but Ruth was left alone in the situation.

Ruth's future was against her

She knew that she was going to assist Naomi in a strange land with a different language. Why should she travel to a place where she did not know anyone? She was not worried about whether the people would receive her or not. Ruth's concern was to forget about her pain and help someone.

God rewarded her by granting her a husband in the person of Boaz. They brought forth a baby and named him Obed, who became the father of Jesse, who brought forth David, and through the line of David came Jesus, our Savior. When you do something for others, God in turn will bless you.

A great man of God was traveling to help one of his assistant pastors. Looking at his hectic schedule, he should not have worried himself flying to another city to support a member of his staff, but he did it so God could bless him. At the airport he was met by someone who asked him if he could get his address because he felt led by God to give him some money. He later on sent to the preacher $70,000 dollars. If this pastor had not been willing to go to support his assistant pastor, he would have missed this great blessing. When we help others, we open our lives to the blessings of God. When we close our hearts and minds, we block the flow of blessings.

Roadmap # 2
Always keep a great attitude. Even when people forget your deeds,
God will not forget your works.

Esther 6:1-3 and 10-11 [1]On that night could not the king sleep, and he commanded to bring the book of records of the

chronicles; and they were read before the king. 2And it was
found written, that Mordecai had told of Bigthana and Teresh,
two of the king's chamberlains, the keepers of the door, who
sought to lay hand on the king Ahasuerus. 3And the king said,
what honour and dignity hath been done to Mordecai for
this? Then said the king's servants that ministered unto him,
There is nothing done for him.

10Then the king said to Haman, Make haste, *and* take the
apparel and the horse, as thou hast said, and do even so to
Mordecai the Jew, that sitteth at the king's gate: let nothing fail
of all that thou hast spoken. 11Then took Haman the apparel
and the horse, and arrayed Mordecai, and brought him on
horseback through the street of the city, and proclaimed
before him, thus shall it be done unto the man whom the
king delighteth to honor!"

Mordecai, the uncle of Queen Esther, had once supported the king by giving him a tip. Certain of the King's enemies were plotting against the kingdom. They could have carried out their plans if Mordecai had not informed the king. This was a great thing that was done by Mordecai. The kingdom was secured, and the king was safe, but nothing was done for Mordecai for several years. It was because of what Mordecai did that Haman, his enemy, had a job in the palace. Why was this so? If the kingdom had been taken over by the two enemies of the King (Bigthana and Teresh), Haman would not have had a place to work.

Mordecai did what needed to be done though he had been paid evil for what he had done. When Haman planned to kill all the Jews, he had no idea what the Mordecai had done for the kingdom, and the night before he was going to kill the Jews, God, through His divine means, caused the king to read about what Mordecai had done, and he was rewarded accordingly. God knows what we do and our payday will come!

Roadmap #3
Do not despise your gift because it has no title, or honor. God has performed miracles with little things.

Have you ever noticed how God uses little things? David's sling, Moses' rod, and the widow's mite come to mind immediately. Someone once said, "Little is big if God is in it." Paul tells us that, "*God hath chosen the weak things of the world to confound the things which are mighty.*" Why? So "that no flesh should glory in His presence."

Roadmap # 4
Learn how to seize opportunities.

I Samuel 17:22-26 And it came to pass, when the Philistine arose, and came and drew nigh to meet David, that David hasted, and ran toward the army to meet the Philistine. [49]And David put his hand in his bag, and took thence a stone, and slang *it,* and smote the Philistine in his forehead, that the stone sunk into his forehead; and he fell upon his face to the earth."

When David was sent by his father to serve food to his brethren, his father told him to bring back a report. David went with his weapon in his hand. He did not wait to go to the battlefield and come back to prepare. No. He seized the opportunity to serve food as a way to fight Goliath.

If you study the life of David you will find that he had been killing animals all along in the desert but he was not qualified to kill Goliath. David used the occasion of serving food to his brethren as a way to seize the opportunity to fight Goliath.

Saul himself was not convinced that David could kill Goliath, but here again we see David seizing the opportunity to encourage King Saul to be strong for God will help him to kill the giant, and he did it.

Roadmap #5
Make the most of every opportunity that you find.

14Then Pharaoh sent and called Joseph, and they brought him hastily out of the dungeon: and he shaved *himself*, and changed his raiment, and came in unto Pharaoh" (Genesis 41:14).

32And for that the dream was doubled unto Pharaoh twice; *it is* because the thing *is* established by God, and God will shortly bring it to pass. 33Now therefore let Pharaoh look out a man discreet and wise, and set him over the land of Egypt. 34Let Pharaoh do *this*, and let him appoint officers over the land, and take up the fifth part of the land of Egypt in the seven plenteous years. 35And let them gather all the food of those good years that come, and lay up corn under the hand of Pharaoh, and let them keep food in the cities. 36And that food shall be for store to the land against the seven years of famine, which shall be in the land of Egypt; that the land perish not through the famine. 37And the thing was good in the eyes of Pharaoh, and in the eyes of all his servants. 38And Pharaoh said unto his servants, Can we find *such a one* as this *is*, a man in whom the Spirit of God *is*? 39And Pharaoh said unto Joseph, Forasmuch as God hath showed thee all this, *there is* none so discreet and wise as thou *art*: 40Thou shalt be over my house, and according unto thy word shall all my people be ruled: only in the throne will I be greater than thou" (Genesis 41:32-39).

Joseph was called upon to explain a dream for Pharaoh. He could have just explained the dream and gone back to the prison house, but Joseph prepared himself by shaving and putting on new clothes because he was going to make full use of the opportunity. He offered to the king advice that led the king to choose Joseph as his prime minister. Sometimes things do not burst into full bloom at a magic moment. Your current situation may have a wealth of hidden potential. Why not find out?

Roadmap # 6
Do not let your necessities eat up your possibilities.

And Benaiah the son of Jehoiada, the son of a valiant man, of Kabzeel, who had done many acts, he slew two lion-like men of Moab: he went down also and slew a lion in the midst of a pit in time of snow...(I Samuel 23:20).

Sometimes in our lives we become so preoccupied with our present circumstance that we lose sight of the possibility that God has in store for us. Benaiah also was one of David followers; he was able to kill a lion on a snowy day. He could have given up hope because of the cold weather. He chose to fight, and God helped him.

Roadmap #7
People may give up on you, but do not give up on your potential.

Eleazer, one of the followers of David, brought forth victory to God even though everyone deserted him (2nd Samuel 23:9-10). [9]And after him *was* Eleazar the son of Dodo the

Ahohite, *one* of the three mighty men with David, when they defied the Philistines *that* were there gathered together to battle, and the men of Israel were gone away: [10]He arose, and smote the Philistines until his hand was weary, and his hand clave unto the sword: and the LORD wrought a great victory that day; and the people returned after him only to spoil.

Roadmap # 8
Be completely humble.

I Peter 5:5-6 "Likewise, ye younger, submit yourselves unto the elder. Yea, all *of you* be subject one to another, and be clothed with humility: for God resisteth the proud, and giveth grace to the humble. Humble yourselves therefore under the mighty hand of God, that he may exalt you in due time."

James 4:10 "Humble yourselves in the sight of the Lord, and he shall lift you up."

Roadmap #9
Match your Charisma with Character: Live by a code of integrity

Developing a personal code of integrity starts when you commit yourself to guidelines that provide you with a sense of moral control of your life. Such an effort will always guide you to know how to react when temptation comes. Once a person decides to live his or her life with such principles, they will be ready when tests come. They do not need to reconsider or negotiate about what to do. Such a code builds holy conduct into the fiber of your life. This is a kind of lifestyle that our spouses, families, churches and nations are longing for.

Roadmap #10
Be accountable to someone.

Accountability can be formal or informal, but it is essential. Many people are not even accountable to their spouses. Their partners do not know what they are doing or what they are about. The absence of accountability may contribute to leaks in your ability to move forward. Refuse to be a lone ranger. You need friends who can correct you. We all need checks and balances in order to develop good character and to keep from falling.

KEEP YOUR EYES ON THE PRIZE

"Brethren, I count not myself to have apprehended: but this one thing I do, forgetting those things which are behind, and reaching forth unto those things which are before, I press toward the mark for the prize of the high calling of God in Christ Jesus." (Philippians 3:12-14)

My dear friend, one of your greatest struggles is going to be remaining focused on your greatest strength. In order to find a fulfilling life, you must be able to press on toward that "one thing" that the Apostle Paul stressed: the high calling of God in Christ Jesus. That is our one and only calling. How we manifest that calling depends on the gifts and strengths God has given each of us.

"But Pastor Kwame," you might ask, "I have to have a job. I cannot afford to pursue dreams."

It is true that the calling of God might not manifest itself initially as a job. Many saints of God have had to hold down several jobs in order to live and see their dreams prosper. Many times, however, if we remain focused on our calling, the right job will come.

"But how do I know if I am a success?"

We have all sinned and come short of the glory of God; therefore, on one level we are all failures. The richest and most famous sinner in the world is still a sinner. We become successful in overcoming sin by having a right relationship with God. Jesus is the One who has unlocked the chains that had us bound, and He has put us in right relationship with God. That is why it is possible to discover our true identities in Christ. God knows who we really are, and He wants us to reach our fullest potential without hiding behind excuses or being bound by fear.

It is not by our own strength or good works that we become successful; success comes when we work together with God who has given each of us a calling, a destiny, to fulfill.

Be careful how you define success. Success does not always mean having lots of money or things. A big house or a fancy car does not guarantee success. Think of the people you have known who have been wealthy in material things, yet poor in their ability to enjoy life.

Success does not always mean happiness. We all want to be happy and fulfilled. We believe that every person has a right to pursue personal happiness. But Jesus never said He had come so that we could all be happy in the eyes of the world. He came to give us abundant, eternal life. It is wonderful when we are happy; but I would rather have a lasting and abiding joy than to chase happiness that comes and goes.

The joy of the Lord is ours when we are walking in his will, doing those things that He has made us uniquely qualified to do.

"The mind grows by what it feeds on."

—J. G. Holland

Chapter 7

START USING YOUR GIFT

I wrote earlier in this book that you already know what your gift is; you just have to start exercising it. You will be amazed what happens after you take that first step. If your talent is baking tasty cakes, soon after you start baking and let people sample your cakes, many people will want to order a cake from you.

I know a woman named Rose who has a gift for cleaning. Rose lost her regular job along with her health insurance benefits and was forced to go out and start her own cleaning service by herself. Within three months, she had more work than she could handle, and she was planning to hire her first employee. How did Rose do it? When she cleans a house or office, the clients are so pleased that they invite her to do their regular cleaning, and they refer her to others. They know quality when they see it.

A young man I know, Antonio, was working at a Christian radio station. The radio station was bought by a man who allowed many things to happen that were damaging to the station's outreach. Antonio has a natural talent for radio and music. He knows how to produce quality programming. His heart was breaking over the decline of what he knew could be a wonderful ministry that also provides jobs. He wanted to discuss his suggestions with the new owner, but he and the other employees feared for their jobs. Antonio had suffered many years of poverty before he was hired in radio work, so he was especially sensitive to what a life with no job could mean. After he could not stand being silent any longer, he went to the owner with his list of problems and solutions to make the station better. Instead of firing him, the owner made Antonio the new manager of the station. As manager, he was able to implement the needed changes and use his gift for radio. Today, Antonio's radio station is one of the best Gospel music stations in the United States.

Finally let us ponder over these four questions as you make the decision to become what God has ordained you to be.

1. What Makes People Praise You?

Proverbs 27:21 "As the fining pot for silver, and the furnace for gold, so is a man to his praise." According to this passage, the writer wants us to know that in order to use gold and silver, they need to go through the furnace or a process. In the same way the praise that we receive from people is a clue that we are actually becoming what we are suppose to be.

I have found out that often before God promotes someone in the Bible, there comes praise first, Just before Pharaoh promoted Joseph, he praise him (Genesis 41: 38-39). ("And Pharaoh said unto his servants, can we find such a one as this is, a man of whom the spirit of God is? And Pharaoh said unto Joseph, for as much as God has shown thee all this, there is none so discreet and wise as thou art")

David was also praised before the people of Israel. (I Samuel 16:18: "Then answered one of the servants and said, Behold,

I have seen a son of Jesse the beth-lehmite, that is cunning in playing, a mighty valiant man, and a man of war, and prudent in matters, and a comely person and the Lord is with him.")

All these people received praise from the people; however, there is a word of caution here. First and foremost, you should be careful with people's praise because it could lead to destruction. Often people could flatter you and that might lead you astray. Secondly, you must transfer all praise to God. If you fail to give all the glory back to God, you will end up becoming puffed up and consequently lose the gift of God. Do not share the glory of God. This reminds me of something that I witnessed. A great man of God was being introduced to preach and the whole congregation was clapping their hands. The pastor kept telling the crowd to keep on with the clapping and I said to myself, "this man is taking God's glory," but then he told the church, "All the glory goes to God." At that point the praise went on the next level. The man of God had learned to redirect all the praise to God. That is what we should do. We should make it our goal to glorify the father with our gifts. The second question to ponder about is...

2. What Do You Do That Produces Great Joy?

John 3:29 "He that hath the bride is the bridegroom, but the friend of the bridegroom, which standeth and heareth him rejoice greatly of the bridegroom voice, this my joy therefore is fulfilled."

John's disciples drew his attention to how Jesus was gaining popularity. John's reply to this question was very simply, he said to them that his job was mainly to prepare the way for Christ and that was his joy. There is a kind of joy that comes to you not only by accomplishing something but also by the mere fact that you have connected yourself to your calling. In

Matthew 25, when Jesus was talking about the talents that were given to the servants, he told those servants who had worked with their talents that they should enter into their joy. You too can enter into your joy today if you would be faithful to your heart and do the will of God. Jesus overcame great adversity because of the joy of His calling that was set before Him. Hebrews 12:1-2: "Looking unto Jesus the author and the finisher of our faith, who for the joy that was set before Him endured the cross, despising the shame and is set down at the right hand of the throne of God." This kind of joy is connected to one's purpose in life. The amount of joy that you have in a particular direction in your life should alert you to whether you are off track or on track. Do you remember the last time that you did something with the most joyful experience? It could be a clue. The third question to ponder about is...

3. What Keeps You Going

John 4:34 "Jesus said unto them, my meat is to do the will of Him that sent me and to finish His work." Jesus and his disciples had come to the well of Jacob. Jesus, however, was tired and needed to eat and rest so he could be refreshed and keep on with the work of his Father. The disciples were already gone to buy food but Jesus saw that a woman had come there to draw water. Perceiving in his spirit that the woman was ready for God, he ministered to him. When the disciples came to him, they urged him to eat something and his reply surprised the disciples. Jesus became refreshed almost immediately after he finished ministering to the woman. His wariness was gone and now he could move on though he had not eaten anything physically. His destiny kept him going. I challenge you today that as you begin to take this journey of knowing God's plan for your life, it will keep you going.

4. Where Do You Experience Quick Learning And Results.

This is a very difficult area to know because sometimes it takes time for something to really work for you, so you cannot quit too soon and conclude that maybe it was not meant for you. It may be that God is trying your patience. It took King David several years to be installed as a king in Israel after he was anointed as king. Moses had a heart to deliver the people of Israel but he finally fulfilled that purpose after forty years of waiting. The main idea here is to know that several repeated attempts without any results may be a sign that you need to seek the face of God for more confirmation and to reconsider where you are. In addition to this, it is very important to know that if you are outside of God's will, like the prodigal son in Luke 15, you will lose your peace, interest, desire and energy to move on. Once you begin to lose the fruit of the Spirit and your drive, then it is time to hear from God to confirm His plans in your life.

CONCLUSION

My dear friend, I encourage you to put these principles into practice in your life. Do not allow fear or ridicule from others to keep you from the race that is set before you. When the struggle gets difficult, pick up this little book and read any chapter. Read your Bible. Surround yourself with positive people who want to see you succeed.

It is my prayer that you will soon break through all the barriers that have kept you from God's best. All of heaven will rejoice to see the real you come forth, walking in the light of God's love and grace.

Chapter 8

DESTINY SURVEY

Action Steps:

The nine questions below were formulated to help you determine if your life is centered on purpose. In combination with the key points in this chapter they will help you to clearly define and create your life purpose

Read each question and answer "yes"; "don't know/not sure"; or "no".

1. Do you clearly know what God wants you to do?

Jesus made his purpose clearly to Paul. "But rise, and stand upon thy feet: for I have appeared unto thee for this purpose, to make thee a minister and a witness both of these things which thou hast seen, and of those things in the which I will appear unto thee;" Acts 26:16 KJV Paul finished his course.

"I have fought a good fight, I have finished my course, I have kept the faith." 2 Timothy 4:7 KJV

Jesus himself knew his purpose. "Pilate replied, "You are a king then? You say that I am a king, and you are right," Jesus said. "I was born for that purpose. And I came to bring truth to the world. All who love the truth recognize that what I say is true." John 18:37 NLT

Yes ☐ **Don't know/not sure** ☐ **No** ☐

2. **Do you know what your potential (Gift, talent, grace, ability, skill etc) is?**

A lot of people don't know but God desires that his children realize their potential. "Now concerning spiritual gifts, brethren, I do not want you to be ignorant" 1 Corinthians 12:1 NKJV

Yes ☐ **Don't know/not sure** ☐ **No** ☐

3. **Do you see fruits in what you are doing right now?**

Sometimes it takes time to see results but if you keep doing something over a period of time and all that you see is frustration and struggles, you may want to reconsider your gift, approach, timing or location. God wants us to bear fruits. "I am the true vine, and my Father is the gardener. He cuts off every branch that doesn't produce fruit, and he prunes the branches that do bear fruit so they will produce even more." John 15:1-2 NLT

Jesus rebuked the lazy servant for the lack of bearing fruits. "But his Lord answered and said to him, 'You wicked and lazy servant, you knew that I reap where I have not sown, and gather where I have not scattered seed. So you ought to have deposited my money with the bankers, and at my coming I would have received back my own with interest" Matthew 25:26-27 NKJV. God gets disappointed when his children produce no fruit.

"Then Jesus used this illustration: "A man planted a fig tree in his garden and came again and again to see if there was any fruit on it, but he was always disappointed. Finally, he said to his gardener, 'I've waited three years, and there hasn't been a single fig! Cut it down. It's taking up space we can use for something else." Luke 13:6-7 NLT

Yes❒ Don't know/not sure❒ No❒

4. **Do you feel God's peace, joy, power and anointing?**

Jesus invited the servant who worked with his talent into the joy of the Lord. "His Lord said unto him, Well done, good and faithful servant; thou hast been faithful over a few things, I will make thee ruler over many things: enter thou into the joy of thy Lord." Matthew 25: 23 KJV
"Then Jesus explained: "My nourishment comes from doing the will of God, who sent me, and from finishing His work" John 4:34 NLT

Yes❒ Don't know/not sure❒ No❒

5. **Do you have confirmation from your family, friends and mature people?**

John the Baptist confirmed the call of Jesus. "But someone else is also testifying about me, and I can assure you that everything he says about me is true. In fact, you sent messengers to listen to John the Baptist, and he preached the truth." John 5:32-33 NLT. Peter had a revelation about who Jesus was. "Simon Peter answered, "You are the Christ, the Son of the living God." Matthew 16:16 NASB

Elizabeth confirmed the words of the angels concerning to her cousin Mary. "For indeed, as soon as the voice of your greeting sounded in my ears, the babe leaped in my womb for joy. Blessed is she who believed, for there will be a fulfillment of those things which were told her from the Lord." Luke 1:44-45 NKJV

Yes☐ Don't know/not sure☐ No☐

6. **Do you feel like you are in the center of God's will for your life?**

   Jesus was successful because he did the will of God.

   "For I have come down from heaven to do the will of God who sent me, not to do what I want." John 6:38 NLT

   Yes☐ Don't know/not sure☐ No☐

7. **Are you using what comes to you naturally?**

   Yes☐ Don't know/not sure☐ No☐

8. **Does what you are doing relate to your potential?**

   Yes☐ Don't know/not sure☐ No☐

9. **Do you feel you are living below your potential (Is there a question mark in your life)?**

   Yes☐ Don't know/not sure☐ No☐

SCORE YOUR RESULTS THIS WAY:

For each **YES** answer give yourself — **0**
NOT SURE or **don't know** scores as — **1**
Each **NO** answer scores a — **2**

Now add up your score. There are no right and wrong questions. However, by using the score analysis it would help you to reduce frustration and help you to be more focus on the most important things in your life. Here is how it works:

If you score between 0-6 you are in the very center of God's will.

If you scored between 7-12, you have a sense of purpose but you need to do soul searching as to where to spend most of your time.

If you scored 13-18, you have not tapped into the plan of God for your life. You have the opportunity to spend time with God so He would make His plans known to you.

About The Author

Kwame Frimpong

Kwame Frimpong Nyanor is the pastor of PowerHouse International Church, Marietta Georgia, and founder of breakthrough today, a teaching ministry with the purpose of reaching the world for Jesus Christ through the media. Pastor Kwame attended Action Faith Bible College in Accra-Ghana, whose chancellor is Bishop Nicholas Duncan-Williams. He is an ordained minister. Currently, he is continuing his studies at Liberty University. Pastor Kwame is an insightful Bible teacher, songwriter and passionate motivational speaker. His heartfelt desire is to see believers discover and fulfill their individual callings as well as help believers recognize and defeat the enemy in their personal lives and in their churches.

Since 1989, Pastor Kwame has been in full time ministry teaching extensively in Africa, Europe and the United States. Hundreds of individuals and families have benefited from both his Pastoral and Family counseling work. His broadcast teaching ministry on Spiritual Warfare began with Radio and TV in Charlotte NC and is expanding around the world via the internet andinterviews on Christian Talk Shows. Pastor Kwame is originally from Ghana, West Africa, though he has been residing in the U.S.A. for the past 18 years. He currently resides in Charlotte, NC with his spouse, Mary and their three daughters Esther, Gloria, and Edna. He is available to speak at churches, seminars and youth retreats. His upbeat motivational messages include his three books, "Overcoming Offenses", "It's Not Your Fault", and "Breaking Through to the Real You" "Eat the colors Stop the killers" which has blessed many and continues to be a blessing. You can e-mail Pastor Kwame at kwamebook@yahoo.com,info@breakthroughtoday.org or visit him online: www.powerhouseint.org or www.breakthroughtoday.org.